RIGHT-ON
IDEAS
for youth groups

Compiled by
Wayne Rice & Mike Yaconelli

ZONDERVAN
PUBLISHING HOUSE

OF THE ZONDERVAN CORPORATION
GRAND RAPIDS, MICHIGAN 49506

Right-On Ideas for Youth Groups

Copyright © 1973, by Youth Specialties

Fourteenth printing March 1982

Library of Congress Catalog Card Number 73-2658

ISBN 0-310-34951-6

The authors wish to express their appreciation to the many churches, youth groups, and youth organizations whose creativity made this book possible.

Printed in the United States of America

CONTENTS

INTRODUCTION

Congratulations! You have just purchased a book that is absolutely worthless . . . unless you read this chapter carefully.

Right-on Ideas for Youth Groups is a compilation of the best youth programming ideas in use today. Every idea in this book has been used successfully in youth programs all over the country. But possessing a book of good ideas isn't enough. We have found that certain ingredients must be present for an idea to be effective. So before you run out and use the ideas in this book, take time to find out **how** to use them.

THE INGREDIENT OF HUMOR

Many church groups voice opposition to the use of humor in youth programs. We have listed five of the most common reasons given:

1. **Humor Can Only Be Done Well by Certain Personalities**
   What makes a person funny **is** his personality. The important thing is to determine what in **your** personality makes people laugh. All of us can be humorous as long as we be ourselves and do not try to compete with or imitate others.

2. **Our Group Doesn't Respond to Humor**
   There are many reasons a group doesn't respond to humor. First of all, they may not have had anything to laugh at. Or the room may discourage laughter because it's too formal or too large. The best setting for kids is an informal, small room where they can relax.

It may be that your young people are afraid to laugh because they feel that God and laughter don't go together. Whatever the reasons, let's understand that all groups respond to humor if you give them a chance.

3. Humor Is Not Appropriate

Many feel that humor does not fit in a church-related service. They feel it is disrespectful to God and the church. Humor does not always have to be a distraction; it can also enhance a program, as you will see in this book.

4. Humor Is Shallow

Many groups have dismissed any humorous activities as shallow and unnecessary. They say their group feels a need to discuss basic issues rather than waste time with fun and games. We're not suggesting that humor is **necessary**, we only say that used in a balanced program, it is anything but shallow.

5. Humor Is Different in Our Area

Although it is true that certain areas have localized humor, it is equally true that if something is funny most everyone will laugh. The point is, the ideas in this book will work anywhere in this country. They already have.

THE INGREDIENT OF TIMING

The success of every crowd breaker, skit, game or activity depends upon its timing. Anytime young people are involved in a program, it is vital to keep the program moving with no time lags. Here are some helpful hints about timing:

1. Always have all props and equipment readily accessible. There should be no vocal pause while you are hunting or reaching for the necessary equipment.

2. Set time limits for each event. Time limits should be judged by the audience response, not by the hand of the watch. In other words, if the event was to be thirty seconds and the audience is bored, end it early. Call time whenever an activity is dragging or not going over.

3. Know what you're going to do before you begin. Never read off a script, if possible.

4. Always check out the location of the event first. Decide the best seating

arrangement ahead of time. Make sure there is plenty of room for movement without breaking anything.

5. Set up film or recording equipment ahead of time and double check to make sure you have plenty of cord and an available electrical outlet.

6. Use applause and cheering to fill in dead spots. Encourage a general audience response to any activity being performed.

7. Divide group into teams that cheer for contestants or participants. Further motivation can be encouraged by threatening a penalty to the least enthusiastic team.

8. You are not a slave to a schedule or activity. If something is not going over, stop it. If you have chosen three contestants and two have not been effective, cancel the third.

9. Always build to the punch line or ending, but never drag it out. Leave the audience laughing and wanting more. Don't drain them until they cannot laugh any longer.

10. Be selective with both the leader and participants. Don't allow someone to ruin a skit or crowd breaker because he is shy, too slow, etc.

11. Always have an alternative. Be prepared in case something goes wrong with the planned activity and have an alternate plan ready and waiting.

12. Insure success by "fixing" certain stunts. Inform the victim privately of his fate and ask him to go along.

13. Don't rely on kids to run the activities in this book. These are generally activities for them to participate in under leader direction.

THE AUDIENCE INGREDIENT

Every audience is different. As a leader, you must use the audience in the most effective way:

1. Use key people, well-known to the group. If well-known people are participating, the activity will be considered in a more favorable light.

2. Have the group choose the contestants. (Be careful that their choice isn't someone they want to ridicule.)

3. Use leaders or popular adults in the activities. Let the group know the leaders aren't immune from the activities.

4. Take advantage of a loudmouth or attention-getter. Involve him in an activity in which he is the victim and let the audience enjoyment put him in his place.

This book contains the best crowd breakers, stunts, games, skits, and creative communication ideas in use today. Their effectiveness with your group depends on you. We hope you recognize that the contents of this book are meant to be a **supplement** to your youth program. This book was written as a source of workable materials that will help you attract and interest kids in what you have to say. We are not suggesting that your youth programs should be fun times or skit nights. We have assumed that you have a message to give to young people. Hopefully, you have a solid program and philosophy in which you've recognized your responsibility and opportunity to share the Gospel of Jesus Christ with your young people. **Right-on Ideas for Youth Groups** was never meant to be a substitute for the message of Christ. It is to be used, rather, as a means of communication that will reach an otherwise unreachable young person with the hope of salvation and redemption.

CROWD BREAKERS AND SKITS

As far as programming is concerned, the success of any type of meeting is usually determined by what takes place in the first ten minutes. It is during this time that people (young people, especially) get turned on or off to the program and those connected with it. For example, when you turn on a T.V. program, you probably judge the entire show on the first few minutes. If it starts out bad, you simply change channels or turn the T.V. off. But in a youth meeting, kids will usually just turn their brains off.

The Crowd Breakers in this book are designed to be used primarily as "program starters." When properly used, they become effective tools for winning the attention of any group of young people in almost any situation. Crowd Breakers are fun activities which call everyone in the group in either indirect (observance) or direct (involvement) participation, and inevitably result in a lot of laughs and a well-balanced program.

One type of Crowd Breaker is the "Group Participation Activity" in which the entire audience involves actively in an unskilled, non-competitive game. The "World's Largest Volleyball Game" and "Human Bingo" are good examples of this. Both are great games that can be played by the group without leaving their seats and in both cases, everyone is involved. This kind of activity helps each person feel more like an important part of the meeting itself.

Another type of Crowd Breaker is the "Fall Guy Stunt." Examples are the "Carrot Drop" and "Banana Bolt" in which the group watches one of its members receive a crazy consequence of some kind. This provides a lot of laughs and is excellent for warming up an otherwise cold audience. It is often advised to 'fix' these stunts so that a "bomb" is avoided. The "fall guy" is clued in ahead of time that he is going to get it, and the result is a successful Crowd Breaker. "Fixing" is, of course, dependent on individual circumstances and should not be done in every case.

A third type of Crowd Breaker is the "Competition Stunt." The audience watches a contest between two or more people in much the same way as they would observe a football or baseball game. The difference is that the competition is on a much smaller scale and that it is unusual and fun to watch.

Regardless of the "type," the primary purpose of a Crowd Breaker is to make the audience laugh. Laughter is a healthy indication that the crowd is enjoying what is going on and is ready for more.

GAMES AND SPECIAL EVENTS

The key to a successful youth activity such as a social, party, camp, retreat or all day outing is often in the types of games used. When most young people think of "games," they immediately have visions of ping-pong, volleyball or "drop the hanky," which usually fail to turn on the average twentieth-century student.

Games used with today's youth, particularly in a church situation, require most, if not all, of the following characteristics. First, they should be unlike any other game that is typically played by the group at school, home or anywhere else. Kids will then look forward to these games, because they are so unusual and the games will be identified with the program. Whenever the young person remembers the great time he had playing a particularly unusual game, he will also remember the activity, special event, or the youth group.

Good games should also be "unskilled." Many kids feel inferior because they are not athletic or always "come in last," so they refuse to participate in games such as softball or volleyball. However, games like "Killer" or the "Surprise Bag Relay" require no skill or athletic ability whatsoever and everyone is on equal terms.

Another essential ingredient of a successful game is humor. Games should not only be fun to participate in, but they should be inherently funny. For example, the whole idea behind games like the "Great Chicken Race" or "Musical Water Glasses" is that they are totally ridiculous. Although competition is involved, it is not taken seriously, and the game is played just for the fun of it.

The purpose of a game is for total involvement and enjoyment by everyone. If at any time a game is dragging or not going over, it should be immediately stopped and another game or event begun. Games should not be played just for the sake of playing a game.

CREATIVE COMMUNICATION

Communication as it relates to teaching is not indoctrination. It is a two-way exchange of ideas which results in discovery. This discovery can be accomplished in many different ways and a few of those ways are included in this compilation of "right-on ideas."

Discussions are primary sources of discovery and involvement. Discussion is most effective when stimulated by a relevant news or magazine article, story, survey or film presented by the discussion leader prior to the actual discussion. A good example of this is "The Life-Saving Station," in which a hypothetical story is related to the group which demands a response. It is almost impossible to just "let it lie." Discussion is inevitable.

Another approach to discussion is "To Tell the Truth." This approach is especially good with youth groups that don't like to talk much or it is excellent as a warm-up prior to discussion.

It is important to understand that the biggest hindrance to open and honest communication in the church is often the lack of freedom for young people to say that which may not fit within the confines of "correct" theology. The atmosphere of discussion must be one of complete freedom to express that which one believes, regardless of its adherence to what others believe. Therefore, the leader should only be concerning himself with keeping order rather than guiding the group to the "correct" answers. When the discussion period is over, it is then appropriate for the leader to express his thoughts and opinions, but not in the form of preaching or putting down the opinions expressed by the group. When this is done, young people are more likely to arrive at healthy, lasting discoveries that will result in solid Christian growth.

1. CROWD BREAKERS

1. CROWD BREAKERS

LOVE STORY

DIRECTIONS: Assign each of the following directions to individuals in the group, and have each one put down the answer to his or her direction on paper. After this is done, recite the following story, with all the vocal expressiveness possible, and have the individuals fill in the blank phrases with the answers they have written down on paper. (This will entail keeping track of which group member has answer number one, which has number two, and so on, so that the leader can have the right individual respond at the appropriate place in the story.)

1. Name a girl in our group
2. Name a boy in our group
3. Describe what you were wearing the last time your mother complained about the way you looked.
4. Think of your favorite activity, but do not write that down; instead, name what you were wearing the last time you did this activity.
5. Write down the most useless advice you have ever received.
6. Write down a sentence from the television commercial you most dislike.
7. Name or describe the place you were when you last received some money.
8. Name or describe the worst kind of transportation.
9. Name or describe what you would least like to be caught doing.
10. Name your favorite food.
11. Name your least liked food.
12. Name or describe the most unusual drink you were ever offered.
13. Name or describe the most unusual thing a person can do on a rainy afternoon.
14. If you were your teacher, what would you have said about the last test paper you handed in? Write this down.
15. Think of the greatest goof you ever made. Write down what you wish you would have said at the time.
16. Name or describe the most annoying habit your brother (or father) has.
17. Name or describe the worst reason a boy could have for breaking up with his girlfriend.

"Ladies and gentlemen, we welcome you to another exciting and tearful sequence in the soap opera, **As the World Burns.** As you remember, during the previous episodes in the fateful life of our heroine, 1, we saw that her one great desire was to have a date with the hero of her youth, the handsome and debonair, 2. And now the momentous event has become reality for our beloved heroine, for he has indeed asked her for a date! The drama begins as we see him arriving at her doorstep wearing 3. As the doorbell rings, she runs breathlessly to answer it, looking at her lovely self in her 4. As she shyly greets him, her father looks over his evening paper, takes his pipe from his mouth, and says to the newcomer, 5. But mother imposes with a tearful 6. With this, the couple leave to go to 7 by 8. Once there, they quickly engage in 9. Soon they are hungry, so they go to a nearby resturant, where each orders 10, topped with 11, and washed down with 12. Afterwards, their love deepening as the evening sun spread its amber glow across the horizon, they decide to bring a climax to the date by 13. As he brings her home again, she lingers on the doorstep, and turning to him with the intense sorrow of parting, speaks these tender words about their time together, 14. He, holding back the words he wished he were man enough to say, softly whispers, 15. After the date is ended, she runs upstairs to her room, her heart beating rapidly, and calls her best friend to tell her the exciting evening events by reporting, 16. Meanwhile he walks meditatively off into the rising fog. Tune in again tomorrow, when you will hear him say to his younger brother, after returning from the fog, 17.

BROTHER AND SISTER

This game is very similar to the "Newly Wed Game," but instead of newlyweds, use brother and sister couples. They must work together to score the highest points possible to win. The brother is sent out of the room and the sister answers a series of questions about her brother. She records her answers on large sheets of paper. When the brother returns, he sits in a chair with the sister standing behind him holding up her written answers. Matching answers are a score for the couple. Repeat the process sending the sister out of the room. Then tally the scores and award the prize. You will find that their answers are hilarious.

Sample Questions:

Questions to the Sister About Her Brother:

1. What is the dumbest thing your brother has ever done?
2. What is his favorite food?
3. What do you dislike most about your brother?
4. Describe your brother using only one word.
5. What is the meanest thing he has ever done to you?
6. What is his favorite color?
7. What does he spend most of his time thinking about?
8. If you had one wish, what would you wish about your brother?
9. What is his favorite T.V. program?
10. How often does he take a bath?

Questions to the Brother About His Sister:

1. What does your sister spend most of her time doing?
2. If you were your sister, what would you change about yourself first?
3. About how many arguments do you have with her each week?
4. Who obeys your mom and dad best, you or your sister?
5. How old was your sister when she kissed her first boy?
6. What animal is your sister most like?
7. What is your sister's favorite subject?
8. Does she keep her room clean?
9. How long does she usually talk on the phone?
10. Does she chase boys?

"THERE'S A B'AR !"

Get a few kids to line up in a straight line, shoulder to shoulder, with the leader at the right-hand end of the line. All should be facing the audience if done before a group. The leader then says, "There's a b'ar!" (bear) and the kids are instructed to say, "War?" (where) and the leader responds with, "Thar!" and points to a spot off to his left, but with his **right** arm. The kids are instructed to point also, and keep pointing. Again the leader says "There's a b'ar!" The kids reply, "War?" and the leader says, "Thar!" and this time points to his right with his **left** arm. The kids do the same and now have both arms pointing (criss-crossed). The same things are repeated, this time with the leader squatting and pointing with his left leg to the right. All the kids do the same. Once more the same is repeated and the kids must point with their **noses** to the left. So now the kids are squatting on one foot with their arms crossed and their heads turned to the left. The leader then gives the guy next to him a push (while their heads are turned the other way) and the result is that the entire line will fall like dominoes.

BACK BREAK

A guy comes to the front and lies down across the seats of three chairs, supported at his head, rear end, and his feet. He then must remove the middle chair (under his rear end) and lift it over his stomach and replace it under his rear end from the other side while remaining supported only by his head and feet. If any part of his body touches the floor, he loses and gets a penalty. Have three guys do it for the fastest time.

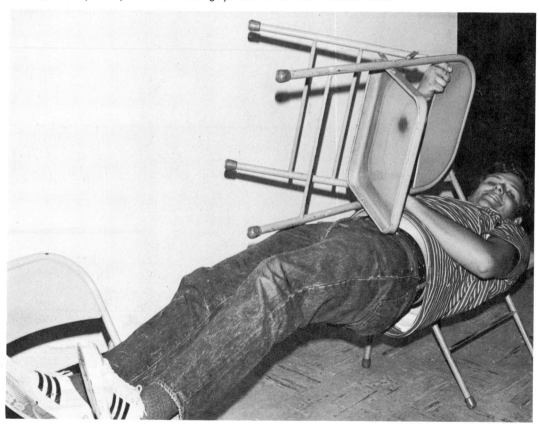

BATACA BATS

A pair of these soft (but durable) red padded bats may be purchased at sporting goods stores or in well-stocked toy stores. If you can't find them in your town, write Bataca, Inc., 550 E. 1st St., Beaument, California 92223 for information. The bats vary in shape, size, and price. Some are filled with air and are quite inexpensive. The best are made of a soft cushion covered with canvas and cost in the neighborhood of $15.00 a pair. Two people can really beat on each other (like a boxing match) without any possible injury or pain. They work great for crowd breakers which call for the use of rolled-up newspapers (e.g. The Newspaper Whomp).

WHAT'S ON YOUR MIND?

Bring three couples to the front of the group and explain that an experiment in "mindreading" is about to take place. (Make a big deal about the implications of ESP, Communications, etc., just to make it interesting.) The guys are told to turn around, backs to the audience and the girls are shown a word (any word of 5-10 letters in length). At a signal, the guys turn around and the girls write the word on the guys' foreheads with the end of their fingers. The guys try to guess what the word is by "feel," as the girls "write." The first guy to figure it out is the most "perceptive" and wins.

To get a good laugh out of this, do it three of four times, and on the last time, put lipstick or soot on the girls' fingers when you give them the "word."

APPLE CHOMP

Two couples are brought forward for an apple-eating contest. Two apples with stems are each tied onto pieces of string. Both couples are blindfolded. The apple is hung down between each couple (they face each other) and at a signal, are instructed to bite the apples. When they start to bite the apples, the person(s) holding the strings pull the apples up and the couples bite each other.

BELLY-WHISTLE

Announce that you have invited a great new talent to your meeting, Mr. Tummy Tootwhistle, to perform a musical number. Mr. Tootwhistle comes out. He is a guy who has a giant hat, covering his head, arms, and shoulders, and has a shirt and bow tie at his waist, with fake arms hanging from his hips. Painted on the guys bare stomach is a face, with the mouth being his navel, giving the appearance that the mouth is in a "puckered" or whistling position. The guy then whistles a tune, making his stomach go in and out, which looks like puffing cheeks. A tape recording of the whistling can be used if the guy isn't able to whistle. This is hysterical to watch and provides a lot of laughs in a meeting.

BOMBARDIER

Have couples come up to front of the group. The guys lie down on their backs and hold a paper cup in their mouths. Each girl must stand over the guy, break an egg and drop the contents into the cup. The girl who does the best job wins.

CARROT DROP

Tie one end of a 2' string around the middle of a carrot so that the carrot balances. Pin the other end to the rear of a guy's pants. The object is to drop the carrot into a milk bottle without using hands.

COMMERCIAL TEST

Wrap a dollar bill around any object that can be thrown; a tin can, a block of wood, chalk eraser, etc. Make a list of commercial slogans, such as: "We Try Harder" or "What do you want, good grammar or good taste?", etc. (no products' names). Then toss the dollar to a kid in your meeting and read one of the slogans. If he can identify the product in 5 seconds he keeps the dollar. If he can't guess, he tosses the dollar to someone else and you read another slogan, and so on. The audience must keep quiet (no helping). The dollar is optional — any prize will do.

BANANA BOLT

Ask for three volunteers, blindfold them, and give each a banana. Explain that this is a contest to see who can peel and eat the most bananas in a minute. Before you say "Go," remove the blindfolds from two of them. Then start and watch one person make a fool of himself by wolfing down the bananas.

WORLD'S LARGEST VOLLEYBALL GAME

This is an excellent crowd-breaker for large groups seated in normal auditorium fashion (with a center aisle). Simply place a volleyball net (or nets) down the center aisle and toss a large beach-type ball or "nerf" ball out into the audience. Everyone remains seated, and must hit the ball over the net to the other side. Regular volleyball rules prevail, except no one "rotates." This of course is a little difficult to play when you have a low ceiling, but in most cases, it is a winner of a way to involve the whole audience.

WORLD'S LARGEST SOFTBALL GAME

This is similar to the "World's Largest Volleyball Game" in that you involve your entire audience in the game. Again, you need a center aisle. The "pitchers mound" is in the center aisle. The audience is the outfield. Everyone is an outfielder. In a typical "audience versus staff" game, someone from the audience is elected as pitcher and catcher. Home plate is on the stage or platform. The "staff" is at bat all the time. The pitcher throws the ball (a soft mush-ball or "whiffle" ball) over home plate and the batter hits the ball into the audience. The batter then must run to a certain point and get back to home plate before the audience can get the ball back to the catcher. (Usually the batter runs to the pitcher's mound and back to home, but the pitcher cannot tag him "out" if he gets the ball.) If the batter. gets back to home plate before the ball does, the "staff" gets one point. If he is tagged "out" by the catcher, the audience gets one point, and so on. When someone catches the ball out in the audience, he stands up and throws it home, or relays it up to home. Everyone else remains seated. The batter is not "out" if someone catches a fly ball. Be sure that the ball is nice and soft, to prevent damage or injury, etc. Toy stores carry a great foam-rubber ball made especially for indoor use.

2. GAMES

2. GAMES

THE POINT GAME

Read a list similar to the one below and each person keeps track of his "points" as specified. Person with the most points wins. Sample list:
1. 10 pts. if you are wearing red.
2. 10 pts. for every penny you have in your pocket.
3. 10 pts. if you have a white comb.
4. Your shoe size in points. 1/2 sizes get next highest points.
5. 15 pts. if your birthday is on a holiday.
6. 10 pts. if you have ridden on a train.
7. 10 pts. if you have a ball point pen; 25 pts. if it has red ink.

SURPRISE BAG RELAY

Divide into teams with ten people on each team. Have a brown paper bag for each team with the following items in each:

Jar of baby food
Green onion
Can of Pepsi (warm)
Raw carrot
Box of raisins
Piece of cream cheese (wrapped
    in wax paper)
Box of Cracker Jacks
Peanut butter sandwich
An orange
An apple

On signal, the first member of each team runs to their bag and must eat the first item he pulls out. Sponsors should make sure items are satisfactorily finished before the person goes back and tags the next member of the team.

THIRD DEGREE

The leader divides the group into two teams, one composed of FBI members, the other of spies. Each spy is given a card bearing one of the instructions listed below, each spy receiving a different instruction. The FBI members then take turns asking questions of specific spies, calling out the name of each spy before asking the question. The FBI members may ask as many questions of as many or few spies as they decide, and may ask any questions they wish (except about the instructions the spies were given). Each spy must answer each question asked him, but always in the manner described on his card. Whenever a spy's instruction is guessed correctly by an FBI member, he is eliminated from the game. The questions continue until all the spies' instructions are guessed correctly. If a spy gives an answer without following his instructions, he is eliminated.

Scores are kept on individuals rather than teams. The winning spy is the one who has the most questions asked him before his instructions are guessed correctly. The winning FBI member is the one who guesses correctly the most number of instructions. (An FBI member may make a guess at any time, whether it is his turn to ask a question or not.)

1. Lie during every answer.
2. Answer each question as though you were (name of adult leader).
3. Try to start an argument with each answer you give.
4. Always state the name of some color in each answer.
5. Always use a number in your answers.
6. Be evasive — never actually answer a question.
7. Always answer a question with a question.
8. Always exaggerate your answers.
9. Always pretend to misunderstand the question by your answer.
10. Always scratch during your answers.
11. Always insult the questioner.
12. Always begin each answer with a cough.
13. Always mention some kind of food during each answer.
14. Always mention the name of a group member during your answers.

START

GIRL ON MATTRESS

BOYS
PASS MATTRESS

MATTRESS RELAY

This game is excellent for camps or large groups. The group is divided into two teams. The boys lie flat on their backs on the floor, side by side, alternating head to foot.

The girls are transported over the line of boys on a mattress and jump off at the end. The mattress is then passed back and another girl gets on. If one falls off, she must get back on the mattress where she fell off. The object is to see which group of boys can transport their girls over themselves the quickest.

This works best when the boys are mostly senior high and when they use only 15 girls. The lighter the girls, the better.

MUSICAL WATER GLASSES

Give each team 8 water glasses, 3 spoons and a pitcher of water. Five minutes are given for the teams to put appropriate amounts of water in each of the glasses forming a musical scale and then practice a song using the spoons to tap the glasses. Points may be awarded for best pitch, best song, best harmony, etc. It is best to put the teams in different corners of the room so they can hear what they are doing.

BROOM JUMP RELAY

Divide into teams. Team members should stand two abreast. First couple of each team is given a broom. At signal "go" the couple must each grab one end of the broom and run back through their team (broom is held just above floor). Everyone in the line must jump over the broom. When couple reaches the back of the line they must pass the broom back to the front of the line. This is done by hands only — no throwing. Then second couple repeats, etc. Game is won by the first team with its original couple again heading the team.

CRAZY FOOTBALL

Team 1 lines up in single file. The first in line is the "kicker." The other team (Team 2) scatters around the field. As soon as the ball (kickball) is kicked, someone on Team 2 gets the ball and everyone lines up single file behind him. The ball is then passed over their heads (or between their legs) until it reaches the last person. Meanwhile the kicker on Team 1 runs around his teammates and they yell each lap. An out is made when the team in the field passes the ball the entire length of the team **before** the kicker makes one lap around his team.

GIANT VOLLEYBALL

Two teams of any number can play this funny volleyball game which uses a giant weather balloon for a ball. Six to eight feet in diameter, the balloon is inflated with a vacuum cleaner. The entire team gets under the ball and pushes it over the net. The opposing team returns it. Giant weather balloons are available from Army surplus stores for about $3.00 each. The eight foot size may be ordered from Edmund Scientific Company, 150 Edscopt Bldg., Barrington , New Jersey 08007 as stock number 60, 568. Price is $6.00 for three balloons and allow two weeks delivery.

HUMAN BINGO

Here is a fun way to break the ice and learn everyone's name. Give each person a Bingo card (below). The blocks are filled in with the names of the persons who fit the descriptions. Each person must sign his own name. The first person to complete all five blocks gets Bingo.

Directions: Fill in the blocks on the next page with the names of persons who fit the descriptions in each box. These persons must be present. The object, of course, is to complete the Bingo Card, either vertically, horizontally, or dia – gonally. Good Luck!

Someone with a pimple	Someone with 3 brothers	Someone with blond hair at least 12" long	Someone who plays football	Someone born out of the U.S.
Someone who owns a dog	Someone who is wearing contact lenses	A foreign student	Someone who is bald	Someone who owns a motor-cycle
Someone with red hair	An amateur photographer	Sign your own name	Someone who got an A in English	Someone who has a snake
Someone who has been in Canada	Someone who weighs over 200 lbs.	Someone who owns a Volkswagen	Someone who has a leather bracelet	Someone who just ate at McDonalds
Someone who went to the World's Fair	Someone who weighs under 100 lbs.	Someone who owns a horse	Someone wearing blue socks	Someone who had a bad date last weekend

KILLER

This is a highly successful game that is great for small groups of less than forty people. Everyone sits in a circle (in chairs, or on the floor) and faces in. The leader has a deck of playing cards and he lets everyone in the room take one card without showing it to anyone. (There are only as many cards in the "deck" as there are people in the room.) One of the cards is a "Joker," and whoever draws it becomes the "killer." No one, of course, knows who the killer is except the killer himself. Play begins then, by everyone just looking around at each other and talking casually. The killer "kills" people by **winking** at them. When a person notices that he has been killed (winked at) he **waits ten seconds** and then says, "I'm dead." The object is to try and guess who the killer is before you get killed. Once you are winked at, you are dead and you can't reveal who did it to you. If you take a guess, and guess wrong, then you are dead too. The killer tries to see how many people he can pick off before he gets caught. When he **is** caught, the cards are collected, shuffled and the game is repeated as many times as there is time.

ARTISTS' IMAGINATION

Divide into teams. Each team should have available a pencil and several pieces of paper. One member of each team is sent to the middle of the room where the leader quietly whispers one item that each must draw upon returning to their group. On signal, each representative returns to his team and without talking or voicing any sound, begins drawing. Team members try to guess what the "artist" is drawing. The first team to shout out the correct item receives 50 points, the second 25. The "artist" cannot write any words in his drawing, only pictures. Items to sketch could include:

Marcus Welby
a pizza
a paper clip
your youth director
a mirror
a tube of tooth paste

the White House
a coffee pot
a telephone
a banana split
the three bears
a gallon jug of root beer

CRAZY BASKETBALL

Divide your entire group into two teams with any number of players. The game is played on a regular basketball court, but without regular basketball rules. In this game, anything goes. The object is to score the most baskets any way you can. You can run, pass, dribble, or throw the basketball with no restrictions. All that matters is to make a basket. Kids can ride piggy-back for height. This game works best with 50 to 200 participants.

PULL OFF

Boys huddle together in any position and lock arms. Girls attempt to pull boys off any way they can.

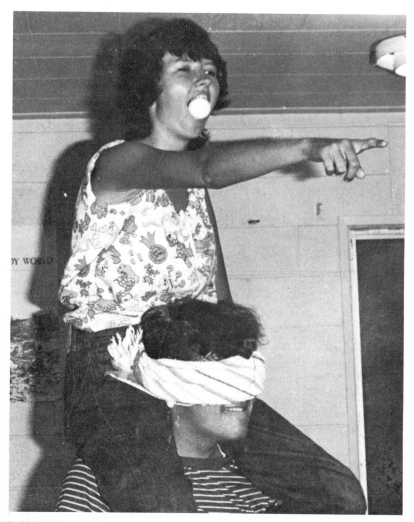

GREAT CHICKEN RACE

This is a relay in which couples participate. The girl jumps on the back of a blindfolded guy and runs him through an obstacle course by giving him any directions she can. To make it a bit more difficult, she is handicapped by having a raw egg in her mouth. If she breaks it, it messes up both her and the guy.

MUSICAL GUYS

Played exactly like musical chairs, except guys are used in place of chairs. The guys form a circle facing center on their hands and knees. Girls (always one more girl than boys) stand behind guys and at the start of the music begin walking in circles around the boys. When music stops, girls **grab** any guy and jump on his back. Extra girl is out. (However, girls are encouraged to fight for their "chair.") Losing girl is eliminated and each new game, one more guy is taken out of the circle.

YARN GUESS

This is one of those things you do just for fun. On one side of the room, put some numbers on the wall (on cards or just write on the wall). Attach to the number the end of a long piece of yarn. Then hang the yarn up the wall, across the ceiling, and down the opposite wall to a letter on the wall. Let the yarn make a few turns, go through things etc., to make it interesting. With about 25 different lengths of yarn going across the room connecting numbers and letter, it really looks wild. The object is to have the kids try to figure out which number connects with which letter. Whoever guesses the most right wins a prize.

FRIS BALL

The game is played like softball with any number of players. A frisbee is used instead of a bat and ball. Also, each team must get six outs instead of three. Frisbee must go at least 30 feet on a fly or it is foul. The offensive team does not have to wait until defensive team is ready before sending "batter" up to plate. (This keeps the normal between innings slowdown to a minimum.)

SKI RELAY

Construct "skis" out of plywood and nail old shoes (from the Goodwill or Salvation Army) to them. Divide your group into teams and each member of the team must put on the "skis", ski (walk, run, or . . . ?) to a pole, go around it and return. Walking with skis is a riot to watch, and going around the pole is really tough with long skis.

THE NOSE KNOWS

Put a dozen or so milk cartons on a table with various smelly things in each. Cover the top with cheesecloth or a nylon or something that will hide what's in the carton, but still let the odor through. Number the cartons and let everybody take a guess, by putting their guess on paper. Announce the winner later on in the meeting, also announcing the smelly goodies. (Please see list of suggestions on page 41.)

Some samples:

Rotten Egg
Ammonia
Coffee
Mouthwash
Horseradish
Smelly sock or gym shorts
Fertilizer
Toothpaste
Pizza
Paint Thinner
Cigarette Butt
Fingernail Polish

```
           3 4 5 6 7 8 9 10 11 12
         2                       13
        1
  GOAL                      GOAL
        1
         2                       13
           3 4 5 6 7 8 9 10 11 12
```

BROOM SOCCER

The chairs are arranged in an oval open at both ends. An equal number of kids sit on the two sides. Each kid is numbered. And each kid has a counterpart on the other side of the oval. The two kids numbered 1 come to the center and each is given a wooden broom. A rubber or plastic ball is tossed into the middle and the game begins. The kids try to knock the ball through their opponents goal (each team is assigned one of the two open ends of the oval). The referee at anytime (as rapidly as he wants) can shout a new number. The number 1's give their brooms to their team mate. Play is in as long as the ball is in the oval (no stopping to change players). If the ball is knocked out of the oval, the **referee** returns it to play. Seated players may not in any way participate.

41

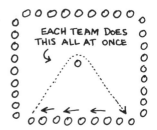

BANANA RELAY

This is a good indoor relay game that requires very little space. Divide group into 4 equal teams and arrange chairs in a square, each team being one side of the square. There is also a chair in the center, but no one sits in it. The first player at the left end of his line is given a banana. (The first player on each team.) At the signal, the first player runs to the center around the center chair without touching it and back to the right end of his own line. In the meantime, all of his team members have moved up one seat toward the head of the line leaving a vacant chair at the right end. After taking the vacant chair, first player passes the banana up the line. When the end player receives it, he repeats the run around center and comes to the end taking the vacant chair. Each team attempts to be the first to have all players circle center chair and get back in original position. Original first player must eat the banana when his team is finished, and his team wins.

PULL UP

Everyone gets a chair and forms a circle, everyone sitting in his chair and facing the center of the circle except for 5 boys and 5 girls who start the game. (They are in the middle, standing). At a whistle the 10 boys and girls in the center of the circle run to the people sitting in the chairs and "pull up" a person of the opposite sex, by taking their hands and pulling them out of their chair. For example a boy would go up to a girl, pull her out of her chair and then **take her seat.** The girl can offer no resistance. She then runs to the other side of the circle, pulls a guy out of his chair, and takes his seat, and so-on. This continues for one minute, the whistle blows, and everyone stops where they are. The boys and girls left standing are counted. If there are 2 more girls than boys, the boys get 2 points, and the game continues. Everytime a minute goes by, the whistle blows and those standing are counted. The idea is sort of a random "musical chairs," boys against the girls. The team with the least left standing each time wins.

42

FICKLE FEATHER

The group kneels and surrounds a sheet that they hold out flat by its edges. A feather is placed in the center. The object is to blow the feather to avoid being touched by it.

3. CREATIVE COMMUNICATION

3. CREATIVE COMMUNICATION

BODY LIFE

Have everyone form a circle or a line, boy-girl, boy-girl. If in a circle they should be facing inward. Give each person a 3 foot piece of string and ask him to tie one end around his left hand and the other around the right hand of the person standing on his left. After everyone does this, everyone will be tied together. Then give the group a project which requires cooperation and time. One example is to walk into the dining room, sit down around a table, pour "kool-aid" into glasses for each person, pass out cookies, say grace, eat and drink, walk to the kitchen and each person wash his own cup and plate. Then cut the string, form a circle on the floor or around a table and discuss what feelings each one experienced during the experiment and why. Ask them what they thought the purpose was and then, how this related to being in the "Body of Christ," what problems, joys, principles did the experiment surface. You might close by reading Romans 12 or I Corinthians 12.

A STICKY SITUATION

This is an object lesson to demonstrate the need for Christian study. It takes as its central idea 2 Timothy 2:15.

Prior to the meeting a stick of any length is prepared and bound with spirals of masking tape. Only you know the exact length (it should be whole inches not 1/4's or 1/2's). To begin the discussion you ask the group to describe the stick as to shape, size, color, texture, anything that might be a clue as to its identity. Next you ask all of them to come to where you have placed the stick on a table or chair, and without touching the stick in any way or using any known measurements try to decide the true length of it by just looking at it. After five or ten minutes divide the group according to their conclusions as to the length of the stick. (For example: all who believe it to be twelve inches in one group, fourteen inches in another group, etc.) After the group is divided, you then tell them to try to convert everyone who is in another group to their group; allow ten or fifteen minutes. This will get loud and amusing. Let it. That's part of the lesson. After time is up, divide them up into groups again just as before, but watch for those who have changed groups. Then starts the real lesson. The leader needs to ask what some of the problems were that they encountered while trying to convert others to their way of thinking. Usually someone says that they didn't know the length of the stick because it couldn't be measured, so they couldn't really convert people. Then ask the ones who changed groups why they changed. You can ask the ones who were certain of the length why they were so positive. The results are interesting and serve as a springboard to launch your group into gaining more knowledge of their own Christian witness. Wait until your discussion is completely over before revealing the true length of the stick.

YARN SHARING EXPERIENCE

In order to get your group to open up and share their inner feelings and Christian experience, try using this technique. Take a ball of yarn (size is determined by the size of the group involved) and explain to the group that you are going to ask them to participate in a little experiment. Tell them that in a moment you are going to throw the ball of yarn (while holding on the end so that the yarn will unwind) to someone in the group. (The group should be standing in a circle). When that person catches the ball of yarn, he should share either 1) What God has done for him, 2) What God has done for someone he knows, 3) What God has done (Christ's death, the Bible, etc.), or 4) Something that he is thankful for. Then after he has shared one of the above, he will throw the ball to someone else in the circle (while holding on to the yarn) and the next person who catches the ball will also share one of the four areas above. You keep this going until everyone in the group has had a chance to share at least once (several times is best, but this depends on the size of your group and the time and interest).

After you have made a spider web like pattern with the yarn and everyone has had a chance to share, stop the ball and begin to ask some questions:

1. What is this yarn doing for us physically? Answers would range around the idea of "holding us together." (Before this you could comment that the effect of the sharing has created a somewhat beautiful web between the members of the group.) You could briefly mention that for a beautiful pattern to evolve, everybody had to participate.

2. Have one or two members of the group drop his hold of the yarn. Immediately the center web comes loose and the effect is for the circle to widen a little. Then ask: "What happens to the group when someone drops their yarn?" (It becomes less close — looser knit and it makes something beautiful fall apart and turn ugly.) You then could follow-up with a brief talk on how the Bible teaches us to bear each other's problems, to share our happinesses and sorrows, to be thankful, etc. You could really emphasize that in sharing, a beautiful network of relationships and ties are formed just like what is physically illustrated by the yarn, but that it takes everyone to hold it (or get it) together. Another possibility is to emphasize the Body concept in I Corinthians 12 and Ephesians 4.

DECISION

Kids have ten minutes to decide which of the following things they consider to be the most harmful. Their job is to rank order each one using the number 1 by the one they think is the most harmful; number 2 by the second most harmful, etc. Afterwards, discuss the results. Define "harmful" as it relates to all areas of life.

_____Getting drunk

_____Moderate drinking (alcohol)

_____Lack of exercise

_____Cigarette smoking

_____Guilt feelings

_____Poor eating habits (types of food, how eaten, etc.)

_____Marijuana

_____Drugs (amphetamines, LSD, etc.)

_____Overwork

_____Premarital sex

_____Lack of medical attention when necessary

_____Nervous anxiety and tension

_____Fatigue, caused by never getting enough sleep

_____Over eating

(You can add others)

TO TELL THE TRUTH — Meeting Ideas

This is a great program idea for an entire meeting that is both highly entertaining as well as extremely productive. The meeting is based on the T.V. game show "To Tell The Truth" and wraps up with a discussion and lesson on "What is Truth" and/or "Honesty and How to Recognize It."

Before your meeting begins, find a boy or girl who has done something unusual or humorous that no one else in your meeting knows about. For example, he may have got lost at Disneyland as a kid, or won a soap box derby, or got sick on a jet plane to Europe, etc. — **anything** that no one else would know about. Then get two other "imposters" who will pretend that they did the same thing. Write out an "affidavit" similar to the type used on the T.V. show, which should describe the "unusual event" which the "mystery person" did. The affidavit should be as humorous as possible. To open the meeting, the three kids each come out and state their real name, and tell what they did. For example, the first guy might say, "My name is John Schmuck and I got lost at Disneyland." The second guy says, "My name is Ralph Klutz and I got lost at Disneyland", and the third guy does the same. Then you read the "affidavit" describing (for example) what happened when the "mystery person" got lost at Disneyland. The three kids are then seated at the front and the audience (one at a time) asks them questions to try and figure out "who did it?" For example, someone might ask, "Number one . . . how old were you when you got lost?" and so forth. After about ten minutes of questions the audience gets to vote for who they think did it. A show of hands for each of the three guys is the best way to vote. Ask various people "why" they voted for each particular guy. After the show of hands for each of the three guys, you ask, "Will the **real** (person who got lost at Disneyland) please stand up?" And the real guy does. This concludes the first part of the meeting, which should be carried out as casually and with as much fun as possible.

After the "game," a discussion should be held on the subject of Honesty. Listed below are some sample questions for discussion:

1. What is dishonesty?
2. When is dishonesty justifiable? (Give examples)
3. Is there such a thing as a "white lie"?
4. What is the most dishonest thing a person could do?
5. How can you determine a lie from the truth?

4. SCAVENGER HUNTS

4. SCAVENGER HUNTS

POLAROID SCAVENGER HUNT

This is a great idea for a party or social that is really different. The idea is to divide your group into teams of five or six kids each. Each team is given a Polaroid Camera, two packages of film (8 exposures each), an hour or two of daylight, and a list of pictures to be taken. The teams all go out in cars and must take at least 15 pictures chosen from the list within the time limit. The pictures are given point values rated according to difficulty, and the team accumulating the most points, wins. The folllowing list of rules and directions should be given to each team:

Rules

A. This is a contest between teams to see which team can accumulate the greatest number of points. Points are earned by taking pictures, as described below, of everyone on the team. The point values of each picture are indicated by the number in parenthesis at the end of each picture description.

B. All teams will leave the church parking lot at the same time, equipped with 1) a Polaroid camera, 2) a team photographer, and 3) an impartial adult supervisor-driver.

C. Each team must pick a team name and a team captain. The team captain will determine where the team is to go to take the pictures.

D. All arrangements for all pictures are to be made by the team members — not by the adult supervisor. The job of the supervisor is to take the team where it wants to go, and take pictures when necessary. (Each supervisor is to use his own discretion with regard to bailing his team out of jail.)

E. At least five team members must be visible and identifiable in each picture, unless otherwise designated.

Directions:

Take as many of the following pictures as possible within the time limit. They are rated point-wise according to difficulty, so you will want to consider that as you decide which ones to take. The maximum you can take is 15 pictures. Good luck.

1. Hanging by knees from a tree. (10)
2. Climbing a flagpole (bottom person must be at least 3 feet off the ground). (15)
3. In a storefront window, on a main street, blowing bubble gum. (5)
4. Inside a police car, with the policeman. (15)
5. In an airplane (10) (with a stewardess +5 with a pilot +7)
6. In a bath tub. (10)
7. Under a lighted building clock at 6:22 P.M. (15)
8. Around a tombstone. (5)
9. Three members of your team in a dryer in a laundromat. (10)
10. Standing on the roof of a service station, with the attendant. (15)
11. Making french fries in the kitchen of a restaurant, with the chef. (15)
12. In a boat on the water. (10)
13. Sitting around someone's dinner table at supper. (The family may not be that of a team member, nor are they to be from our church). (10)
14. All members trying on a pair of new white tennis shoes in a department store. (15) (With store manager +5)
15. With at least two people not in your group or from our church in a telephone booth. Total of seven people. (15) (5 points extra for each additional person, not from your team, you can cram in there.)
16. In a wagon. (5)
17. Fishing on a pier with a borrowed fishing pole. (10)
18. Inside an inner tube. (5)
19. Washing a car in a car wash. (10)
20. T. P.'ing a car (not the one you're in).
21. Collecting candy at a home where your team is trick-or-treating. (10)

SHOPSCOTCH

This is a great party or special event idea. Divide the entire group into small groups of five or six each. Each group then gets an envelope with $1.50 in cash and a list of items which they must purchase. The groups are then turned loose in a shopping center and have 45 minutes to obtain all the items. The group with the most items and the most money left over wins. Receipts must be brought back with everything (including items obtained for free). Shoplifting is a no-no. The leader should go to the shopping center ahead of time to make sure that items on the list **can be** obtained. A sample list:

1. One paint card sample
2. Pocket size Kleenex
3. Empty pop bottle
4. A toy
5. Six peanuts in shells
6. One nail
7. Can of fruit juice
8. An apple
9. A pea shooter
10. A travel brochure to the Bahamas
11. One Kernel of popcorn — popped
12. Three inches of chain
13. 1 1/4 oz. of blue cheese
14. One piece of candy
15. Twelve inches of ribbon
16. A bar of soap
17. "Apple Blossom" ·Deodorette
18. 1 1/2 oz. bag of pretzels
19. Toothpaste "Squeeze Keys"

SOUND SCAVENGER HUNT

Divide groups into teams. Give each team a cassette recorder and a blank cassette. Make a list of "sounds" for the teams to find, record and bring back, in order, within a given time limit. Some sample sounds:

1. Dog barking.
2. Siren on a police car.
3. Roller Coaster at amusement park.
4. Somebody playing a tune on a violin.
5. Someone over 65 explaining what "Funky" means.
6. A tap dance.
7. A bursting balloon.
8. Your entire team singing **all** of "Somewhere Over the Rainbow." Have each team play their recording for the entire group. Judge winner after listening to the tapes.

5. SIMULATION GAMES

5. SIMULATION GAMES

PEACEFUL KINGDOM

There's a lot of talk about peace today. Test your group's inclination toward it. Divide groups into six or eight persons. Give each balloons of one color, some string, straight pins, and masking tape. The intent of the game is to have each group blow up balloons and tape them to a wall space before any other group. Each group should appoint blowers, tiers, and a person to take the balloons to the space. The group leader does not tell group what to do with the pins. The interesting thing is to see how a group plans its strategy for getting its balloons to the space. Invariably there will be an all out war on the other groups, some will hide balloons, some will become very aggressive. Discuss the implications of what happened during the experiment.

BLOCKHEAD

A powerful children's game that several church educators are using in many groups is BLOCKHEAD. (Produced by Saalfield Publishing Co., The Saalfield Square, Akron, Ohio 44309)

This game is available at most toy stores, discount markets and large drug stores for less than $1.50. Two to three sets may be needed depending on the sizes of the groups the game is played with. The results of playing this game in the modified version described below, are much like games costing up to twenty times this amount.

BLOCKHEAD is composed of some 20 small wooden blocks of various sizes and shapes. The aim of the game, as produced by the publishers, is to build a precariously balanced pile of these different shaped blocks without causing it to tumble. This is how it is played normally:

1. Dump the blocks on the floor. Players form a circle around the blocks. Use the flat block title "Blockhead" as a base.

2. First player takes a colored block and places it on the base. No succeeding block may touch the base.

3. Second player takes another block and places it on top the first in any manner he chooses.

4. Third player adds a block on the second block, or places it on the first beside the second if he wishes, and so on . . . each player adding a block to the pile.

5. Each player may use only one hand. He must not touch any block except his own.

6. The player who places the block which causes the pile to tumble is out of the game. The game continues until there is only one winner. The play starts from the beginning each time the pile tumbles.

In a revamped, "recycled" procedure the game is played in three phases:

PHASE ONE: Place the players into teams of 3-6 each, with a minimum of three teams and a maximum of seven teams. Play the game as described above. Same rules. Each team will have one minute to decide who will place what block on the pile. If they cannot decide in this time limit, they forfeit their turn. Each team takes its turn in sequence. Each member of a team should have an opportunity to place a block. Continue the game.

PHASE TWO: Immediately go into this phase, keeping the teams as they are already formed. Place one block on the base as a starter. Begin with the winning team from phase one. The play is similar to the last phase. Except this time the team has two minutes in which to agree on a rule which they will impose on the next team. Such as "Before you place a block on the pile, your team must all do five push-ups" or "you must place the small, yellow cylinder block on the pile with your eyes closed . . . and your team may help you . . ." Stress that any rule is possible during this phase. However, it must be an achievable one. The winning team from phase one starts phase two by imposing a rule on the next team; then that team accomplishes their task and have the opportunity to impose a rule on the next team, and so forth. When a team is making their decision as to the rule they will impose, their decision must be unanimous, if someone disagrees he forfeits his turn. Again, the game continues until a team is declared the winner.

PHASE THREE: Again, go immediately into this phase. Announce that all teams are abolished, and that this phase is played entirely as individuals. Working cooperatively together everyone has five minutes to build the pile as high as they can. Each person should have a turn in placing blocks. Announce when the five minutes are up.

DISCUSSION POSSIBILITIES

1. Ask the group to compare their feelings in each of the three phases. What was happening? How were decisions made? Leadership? Was their team "out to get" another team?

2. What does each phase simulate or model from the real world? Which phase is most like their school classroom, family, community, church . . .?

3. What does each phase say about the nature of man? Which one is most appropriate for the future? How can we bring it about at a personal level?

4. How would you redesign this game, expanding it, changing it so it models an alternative future that might be more appropriate for man to live in? Do it!

RED-BLACK SIMULATION GAME (Discussion on Competition and Trust)

Actually this is more of a learning experience than a "game." Although a game of sorts is involved, the object is to point out the importance of **trust** in our lives, and also to help kids understand their natural tendency to compete and to win, even when winning is not our goal.

THE SIMULATION GAME

(1) The only props needed are about 20 3 x 5 cards, two pencils, and some play money. Play money may be obtained from a Monopoly set, etc.

(2) Have everyone in the group get into two groups. (Avoid using the word "team" as it implies competition.) It might be a good idea for you to explain that an experiment (rather than a "game") is about to take place. The kids can number off 1,2,1,2, etc. or they may just divide up any way they please.

(3) Give the following instructions: **"Each group will have nine opportunities to choose a color, either red or black. The choices are worth money. Here's the way it works: If both groups choose 'black,' both groups will get three dollars. If both choose 'red,' both will lose three dollars. But if one group chooses 'red,' and the other group chooses 'black,' the 'red' choice gets five dollars and the 'black' choice loses five dollars."** Explain this as many times as it takes until everyone understands.

(4) After basic scoring proceedure is explained, then tell the group that there are two simple requirements to fulfill:

   (a) **"To make as much money as you possibly can.**

   (b) **To not hurt anybody."**

(5) Have the two groups go to opposite sides of the room (or preferably to two different rooms) and decide on their first color choice. You remain in the center with the money.

NOTE: It is important that the two groups not know what each other is doing.

(6) Each group selects a leader (in any manner they wish) who brings his group's decision to you on a 3 x 5 card which you furnish him with. Written on the card should be either "red" or "black." You award money to the groups as per instructions in (3).

(7) Game continues. After the fourth attempt at color choosing, you ask if the groups wish to negotiate. The group can pick one person from the other group. After this, announce that the next choice will be worth 3 times as much money. (Don't announce this change in value until after the negotiating has been done, if they choose to negotiate at all.)

(8) Finish all nine rounds and then get together to discuss what took place, and who made how much money.

THE DISCUSSION:

Ask the entire group's reaction to the following questions.
(a) What was your group's strategy; that is, how did you decide just what color to choose?
(b) Did your group fulfill the game requirements? How? (See #4 above)
(c) Did you trust the other group?
(d) Why did (or didn't) you want to negotiate with the other group?
(e) When did you decide (after which choice) to try and beat the other group?
(f) To beat the other group, did you have to emphasize one requirement over the other?
(g) How did you treat the "minority" voice in your group?

AFTER THE DISCUSSION:

It is suggested that you include the following general points in your concluding remarks or "lesson" from the simulation game:

(1) Both groups became involved in competition even though no mention of competition or of beating the other group was made. This shows man's natural tendency to satisfy his ego with being superior to others, or selfishness and greed. It is this natural tendency that in many ways causes poverty, oppression, and

war in the world. Show through Scripture how Christ came to set us free from this nature. See Romans 3-7.

(2) Trust and Cooperation were essential if both groups were going to benefit. Most human relationships today, however, lack trust or cooperation. (Give examples — politics, business, ordinary friendships). As a result, we find it difficult to trust **God**, because we are afraid He won't keep His word, or that we are not being told the truth. But God has trusted us by making the first move — sending His Son. We have to make our choice also by "trust" or by "faith," believing that surely a decision to take God at His word when He offers us life through His Son, will result in a peaceful coexistence between man and God. (Elaborate on this —) John 3:16, Romans 6:23, John 10:10, 2 Corinthians 5:17, etc.

NOTE: The key to the success of this activity is to what degree the two groups actually compete against each other. You cannot encourage competition at all, however, there are ways to make it even more inevitable. One way is to award (instead of play money) something that is **really** worth something or something that the kids really want, such as candy, or real money (pennies or nickels, etc.).

6. SPECIAL EVENTS

6. SPECIAL EVENTS

INDY 500

This is a special event which can be extremely successful when used with a little creativity. The idea is a sort of "Soap-Box-Derby" in which your entire group is divided into teams (two to four) and races cars which they build on-the-spot. You provide the wheels (baby carriage wheels, skates, etc.), axles, wood, rope, tools, nails, etc. for each team, and they have an hour to build a car. It is best that each team receives the same amount and types of material to start with (an hour or two in a junkyard will produce plenty of material in which to build four cars.) After each team builds its car, they are brought to the "starting line" and are first of all judged. (Best looking car, best painted car, etc.) An obstacle-course is set up and each team races its car around the course. The cars and drivers are pushed by team members. Pit crews are ready to make repairs when the cars fall apart. After the race, a meeting may be held to present awards, guest speaker, etc.

THE WORLD'S LARGEST PILLOW FIGHT

For this event, you will need a gym or a room large enough to accommodate a lot of action (also easy to clean). Each kid brings a pillow from home, and sits on it during preliminary activities. Music, crowd breakers, a speaker, etc. are all good at the beginning of your meeting. At the close, the pillow fight takes place. Boundaries are marked on the floor and no one out-of-bounds may participate. When the whistle blows everyone starts swinging pillows and goes for one minute. When the whistle blows, ending the first period, everyone must sit down on his pillow immediately. The last one to do so gets a penalty. ("Hot SEAT," pie in the face, etc.) Those who have "had it" are given the opportunity to leave the fight. The fight continues in one-minute periods until everyone is pooped-out or his pillow breaks. (If a person's pillow breaks, he is automatically out.) Of course a giant feather mess is left behind, which can be cleaned up with large industrial-type vacuums. In smaller pillow fights, ordinary vacuum cleaners will work. Note: No furniture pillows are allowed (big foam-type) and check to make sure kids don't put rocks, etc. in the pillow cases.

73

GROCERY STORE CAR RALLY

Divide your group into cars. Each car load gets 20 shiny new pennies. Instruct them to buy twenty pieces of bubble gum from twenty different grocery stores and bring back a receipt for each penny spent. Prizes are awarded on the basis of speed and variety. A team can win by doing it in the shortest time or trading in stores that no one touched.

DYE FIGHTS

This is a very successful party or special event that can be a real crowd-drawer. Have all your kids meet out on a playing field or vacant lot and supply them with either squirt guns or water balloons. The water is mixed with food dye, however and therefore when you get hit with water you also get colored, as well (you dye!). This may be done in a number of ways, but usually a big free-for-all is the most fun. At the end, whoever is the least "dyed" wins. To fill up water balloons, put a little dye in the balloon first, then add water. After the fight, have all the kids meet at a local hamburger stand for food. People who see them can't believe their eyes. A variation of this is to use squirt guns and red dye only. A game of cowboys and Indians is then played in which two teams each try to eliminate each other by hitting them with the red water. When you are hit, you are out of the game. Last guy to get hit is the winner for his team.

THIRTY-ONE WAYS TO COOL OFF

Obtain thirty-one dishes of the different flavors of Baskin-Robbin's Ice Cream in the small 15¢ size servings. (A discount is usually available when ordered for a church or youth group.)

Place the thirty-one different kinds of ice cream on a table in a circular fashion placing a spoon in each dish of ice cream. Then give each member in the group a spoon, a pencil, and a list of the different flavors.

Put a different number on each dish than is found on the corresponding list and have them go in a circle sampling each kind of ice cream trying to match this with the names on the list. (It is a surprising, tasty type of entertainment and refreshments!!)

This is suitable for about 25 in a group. If the group is larger, have more tables set up.

OLYMPIC MARATHON

Divide your entire group into teams. Each team gets a copy of the marathon "route" (use the one below as a sample, fill in your own locations) and each team enters the names of its team members in the blanks. A team leader reads the entire "route" to the team prior to starting and explains the rules. The marathon is simply a very complicated relay, which each team must complete, step by step, following the directions on the "route" sheet exactly. A banana is used as a "baton" and is passed on person to person. The entire team is always with the participants in action, cheering them on. The example below was used in a large church building, but this may be used anywhere, such as a camp, etc.

NOTE: Banana must accompany the participant at all times. It must be **handed** to the person who is in the next event. Inside the church, there will be **only** fast walking. Anyone who runs will have to begin his event again. All begin by taking stations. Doubling up will probably be necessary — make it easy for the person to get to his next event. If there are too many people, the overflow is to be taken care of in the number of people led blindfolded (#7). DO NOT begin your event until you have been given the banana!

1. _____ starts behind metal line just outside "starting" door (On sidewalk). He rides tricycle to curb line on alley (passes baton).

2. _____ walks on stilts to first door of Hansen Hall, walks swiftly to top of stairs.

3. _____ sits on top stair and goes down to basement, sitting down, one step at a time. At the bottom of the stairs, he picks up a matchbox with his nose, hops on left foot through first door on the right, to where his teammate is. He passes the matchbox from his nose to his teammate's nose.

4. _____ who just got the matchbox on his nose, says loudly and distinctly,

>   Peter Piper picked a peck of pickled peppers.
>   Peter Piper picked.
>   If Peter Piper picked a peck of pickled peppers.
>   Where's the peck of pickled peppers Peter Piper picked?

5. _____ and _____ do a wheelbarrow race. Stop by door of Room 103.

6. _____ goes into 103, picks up the broom handle, stands it up straight, holds onto it, turns around it rapidly 20 times, sets it down, steps over it.

7. _____ directs _____ blindfolded people through obstacle course and back to room 106 (only directs them by speaking).

8. _____ runs to blackboard in 106, draws a picture of an elephant, and signs his name.

9. _____ stands at bottom of stairs and eats one-half peanut butter sandwich. No liquid may be used.

10. _____ crosses Main street but may not cross if there is a car as near as the "yield" sign. He then shoots and MAKES 5 baskets. Same for return.

11. _____ goes to Youth Department Office and wraps _____ _____ with an entire roll of TP. The wrapped-up person must run out into the hall, then his teammates take off his TP and put it ALL in the wastebasket.

12. _____ grabs sack at bottom of stairs, puts on old clothes at first landing. Carrying the sack, he runs outside, to the corner of Main and Weber, back to the door by the alley. Takes off old clothes just inside that door. Puts them back in a sack.

13. _____ pops balloons **while** walking or sitting, going down steps, to the Pepsi machine.

14. _____ untapes 10¢, buys pop, and drinks it.

15. _____ _____ _____ _____ _____ _____ and _____ (6) team members, in Canteen, make a pyramid. The person on the top has to unpeel and eat the banana without falling.

CARPET-BAGGING

If your youth budget is limited and your youth room looks like a dungeon, spend some time with your kids obtaining carpet fragments or samples. Then have the entire youth group with glue and sewing needle carpet their youth room. Not only do the kids have fun, but they will feel like this is **their** room.

CAR RALLY

This is a new kind of car rally that is unusual as well as competitive. The group is divided into "carloads," each with a car and a driver. Each car is given a sheet of questions which must be answered. The location indicated in the last question on every sheet is a check-point where each car and time is recorded and a new route sheet is given. Each car also receives an emergency envelope that is not to be opened until a specified hour. Winners will be judged by time, mileage and the number correct. The emergency envelope contains the location of the "after-rally party." If the cars finish all the route sheets, then the last location will be the address of the after-rally party. The first car to arrive wins. Below are some ideas for your route sheets. Obviously, each area must write its own.

Sample "Route Sheet Questions"

1. Who made the light pole at Costello and Broadway?
2. What color is the sign on the Executive Car Leasing in Encino?
3. What are the Saturday hours for the Hillview Market?
4. How many lights are on the KMPC towers?
5. Who donated the Gum Ball machine at Ralph's in Sherman Oaks?
6. How many pitching machines are at Buddy's Bat-A-Way?
7. When was Pinecrest School founded, and by whom?
8. In total, how many fountains are there at Coast and Southern Federal Savings? Also the color lights in each of the fountains?

Instructions to Drivers

1. You have a sheet of questions which **must** be answered.

2. The location of the last question on every sheet is a check-point. Here your mileage and time will be taken down and you will be given your next route sheet.

3. Any questions you may have during the rally, ask at the check-point.

4. When you left the church, you received an emergency envelope. This is **not** to be opened until 10:00 p.m.

5. If by 10:00 you haven't finished your final sheet, open your envelope and follow the instructions inside.

6. Your envelope will be checked at every check-point to make sure it hasn't been opened.

7. Winners will be judged by time, mileage, and the number correct.

WATER DECATHLON

This is a great idea for a creative swimming party. Divide into teams with 10 on each team. Ten places around the pool should be numbered (1-10) with the numbers clearly visible. Team members stand at each of the 9 stations and when their turn comes, they must wear a life-guard hat (or some other hat) while participating in the event. The hat must be passed to the next person in line before he or she may perform his event. The following is done by the team members. (Each does a different event, one after the other for time.)

1. Swim across the pool with an egg balanced on a spoon. (If the egg falls the swimmer must retrieve it and continue.)

2. Dive to the bottom of the pool and retrieve a brick.

3. Cross the pool hand-over-hand from a rope suspended over the water.

4. Swim across the pool with a tether ball tied to each ankle.

5. Two contestants have one ankle tied together and must swim in tandem across the pool.

6. Sit in an inner tube and hand-paddle backwards across the pool. The tube must then be placed over a stake before the next team member starts.

7. Dive and swim underwater across the pool. (Side to side.)

8. Dunk the youth director in the pool. (Either have a regular dunking machine or some target the contestant must hit with a ball. The clothed youth director can then be pushed backward off the diving board.)

9. Put on a large pair of pants, buckle the belt and put on a long sleeve sweat shirt. The contestant must then swim across the pool with a beach ball for buoyancy and toss the ball through designated goal posts. When the ball goes through the goal posts, this stops the clock.

The team with the best time wins. Penalty seconds will be given for holding the egg, not making the distance underwater, etc.

7. PUBLICITY AND PROMOTION

7. PUBLICITY AND PROMOTION

POSTCARDS

Printed at the left and below are some creative alternatives to the usual "We Missed You" postcards sent out by Sunday schools around the country. Print these on colored card stock and use them for absentees or for pulling new kids. They will give your group a more personal touch. Better yet, have some of your talented kids design some of your own.

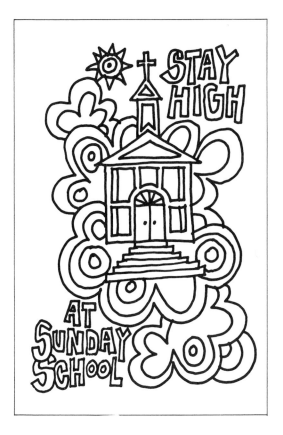

REVERSE ANNOUNCEMENTS

For those who send out publicity notices regularly, and get the impression that some of them are never read, here is an idea.

Place a mimeograph stencil in the typewriter after having folded it back over the top, so that you are actually typing on the back of the stencil. Or, if drawing, you are drawing on the back of the stencil. When printed, everything will read from right to left, instead of from left to right, and all the letters are backwards.

To read this, it will require standing in front of the mirror. The extra effort involved in doing this will almost guarantee its being read.

WARNING ANNOUNCEMENT

Send a postcard one day with the following message: "Tomorrow you will receive a postcard. Read it." It is guaranteed that when you mail the second postcard the next day people will be standing on their heads waiting for it.

MESSAGE IN A CAPSULE

Buy empty capsules at a drugstore. You will probably have to have special permission from the pharmacist (due to drug restrictions). Type three lines, single spaced messages and mimeograph them. Then, cut them into strips, roll them tightly, and put them into the capsule. They are placed into pre-addressed, pre-stamped envelopes. You can imagine how it feels to open a large envelope and find a tiny capsule. The message begins: "Feeling bad lately? Need medicine to pick you up? Here's good news about a picker-upper. Sunday the program will be . . ."

PUZZLED ANNOUNCEMENTS

If announcements have been a drag in your meeting try this: Think up various kinds of word puzzles that have as their answers the details of coming events. There are many types of puzzles that will work — crosswords, etc. Mimeograph them and pass them out at the end of the meeting and the kids must figure out the puzzle to know what is coming up. Post a completed puzzle later on — just in case.

ABSENTEE LETTER

Here's a great idea for a promotional letter to be mailed to all absentees:

Dear _____,

We sure hope xhax you can be wixh us xhis nexx Sunday ax xhe Firsx Bapxisx Church. Because xhis is xhe holiday season, many young people have been gone. We wanx xo keep going xhis summer wixh a boom in axxendance. Come Sunday and lex's go over xhe xop for Jesus.

By xhe way, I guess xhax by now you are wondering why we have lefx oux all of xhe "T's" in xhis lexxer. Xhe reason we have been having so many absenx "T's" laxely, we jusx didn'x have enough xo use in xhis lexxer. DON'T BE AN ABSENTEE SUNDAY.

A PASS-OUT IDEA

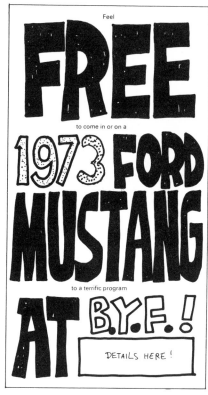

83

ASK SOMEONE WHO KNOWS

The following is the one-and-only truly "All-Purpose" poster idea. No matter what you want to advertise, this poster will do it. It needs no specific information whatsoever. The poster simply reads "Ask Someone Who Knows."

If you are wanting to advertise on a school campus, the poster is hung at various places all over the school, and the kids from your youth group wear a little sticker which reads "I Know."

The principle is fairly simple: Kids around school see a sign that tells them to ask someone "Who knows" and so they ask your kids who are wearing the "I Know" stickers **just what is it that they know.** Of course your kids then can unload all the information about your next meeting or special event and also give the person who asked an "I Know" sticker, because now he knows, too! It is a subtle, but effective means of advertising. It will work also when you have a school that does not allow "religious" or church posters on campus. The poster really says nothing to offend anybody. The posters and stickers can be easily silk-screened.

84

8. SKITS

8. SKITS

THE ART SHOW

Have pictures or paintings hung on a wall at different heights. Have several kids file by the pictures, stopping at each one to look for a moment or to comment to someone about the pictures. All should be dressed in raincoats or overcoats. The final kid comes by inside an overcoat which he holds over his head on a coat hanger (see diagram). A hat is placed over the hook of the hanger. As he reaches each picture he "adjusts his height" by raising or lowering the coat. The effect is hysterical.

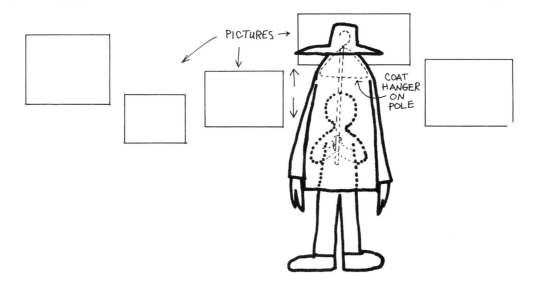

WHO'S ON FIRST?

This is an old Abbott and Costello routine. The lines by themselves will not carry an audience. Good audience response can be achieved by 1) Memorizing the routine (you cannot read this skit) 2) Making sure your timing is precise. 3) Varying the speed and volume of the participants so that the skit climaxes two or three times.

1st man: I understand you used to coach a baseball team.

2nd man: Yes, I did. It was a pretty good team, in fact.

1st man: Were your players good enough to make the big leagues?

2nd man: Well, yes.

1st man: Hey, why don't you tell us some of their names because they might be famous someday.

2nd man: Okay. Let's see, on the bases we have . . . Who's on first, What's on second and I-Don't-Know is on third . . .

1st man: Wait a minute. You're the manager of the team, aren't you?

2nd man: Yes.

1st man: You're supposed to know all the fellow's names?

2nd man: Of course.

1st man: Okay, then, the first baseman's name.

2nd man: Who.

1st man: The guy on first.

2nd man: Who.

1st man: The FIRST BASEMAN.

2nd man: **Who** is on first base.

1st man: I'm asking **you** who's on first base.

2nd man: That's the man's name.

1st man: That's who's name?

2nd man: Yes.

1st man: Look, all I want to know is, what's the name of the guy on first base?

2nd man: No, no, What's on second.

1st man: Who's on second?

2nd man: Who's on first.

1st man: I don't know.

2nd man:	He's on third.
1st man:	Third base? Look. How did we get on third base?
2nd man:	Well, you mentioned the man's name.
1st man:	Who's name?
2nd man:	No, Who is on first.
1st man:	I don't know.
2nd man:	He's on third.
1st man:	Hey, if I mentioned the guy's name, who did I say was on third?
2nd man:	Who is on first.
1st man:	I'm not asking you who's on first . . .
2nd man:	Who **is** on first.
1st man:	I want to know what's the name of the guy on third base.
2nd man:	No. What's on second.
1st man:	Who's on second?
2nd man:	Who's on first.
1st man:	I DON'T KNOW!
both:	Third base.
1st man:	All right. Just forget the infield. Let's go to the outfield. Do you have a left fielder?
2nd man:	Of course we have a left fielder.
1st man:	The left fielder's name.
2nd man:	Why.
1st man:	Well, I just thought I'd ask.
2nd man:	Well, I just thought I'd tell you.
1st man:	Then go ahead and tell me. **What's** the left fielder's name?
2nd man:	What's on second.
1st man:	Who's on second?
2nd man:	Who's on first.
1st man:	I DON'T KNOW!
both:	Third base.
1st man:	Let's try again. The left fielder's name?
2nd man:	Why.
1st man:	Because.

2nd man:	Oh, he's our center fielder.
1st man:	(Exasperated) Look. Let's go back to the infield. Do you pay your guys anything?
2nd man:	As a matter of fact, yes. We give them a little something for uniforms, etc.
1st man:	Okay. Look, it's payday and all the guys are lined up to get paid. The first baseman is standing at the front of the line. Now he reaches out to you to accept his money. Now, who gets the money?
2nd man:	That's right.
1st man:	So who gets the money?
2nd man:	Yes, of course. Why not? He's entitled to it.
1st man:	Who is?
2nd man:	Certainly. Why sometimes even his mother takes the money for him.
1st man:	Who's mother?
2nd man:	Yes.
1st man:	Look. All I am trying to find is what's the name of your first baseman.
2nd man:	What's on second.
1st man:	Who's on second?
2nd man:	Who's on first.
1st man:	I don't know.
both:	Third base.
1st man:	Okay, okay, I'll try again. Do you have a pitcher?
2nd man:	Of course we have a pitcher. What kind of team would we be without a pitcher?
1st man:	The pitcher's name?
2nd man:	Tomorrow.
1st man:	What time?
2nd man:	What time what?
1st man:	What time tomorrow you going to tell me who's pitching?
2nd man:	How many times do I have to tell you, Who is on fir-
1st man:	You say who's on first one more time and I'll break your arm. I want to know what's your pitcher's name?
2nd man:	What's on second.

1st man:	Who's on second?
2nd man:	Who's on first?
1st man:	I don't know.
2nd man:	He's on third.
1st man:	The catcher's name?
2nd man:	Today.
1st man:	Today. Tomorrow. What kind of team is this? All right. Let me set up a hypothetical play. Now. Tomorrow's pitching. Today's catching. I am up at bat. Tomorrow pitches to me and I bunt the ball down the first base line. Today being the good catcher that he is, runs down the first base line, picks up the ball and throws it to the first baseman. Now, when he throws the ball to the first baseman, who gets the ball?
2nd man:	That's the first right thing you've said all night.
1st man:	I don't even know what I'm talking about. Look, if he throws the ball to first, somebody has to catch it. So who gets the ball?
2nd man:	Naturally.
1st man:	Who catches it?
2nd man:	Naturally.
1st man	Ohhhhhh. Today picks up the ball and throws it to Naturally.
2nd man:	He does nothing of the kind. He throws the ball to Who.
1st man:	Naturally.
2nd man:	Right.
1st man:	I just said that. You say it.
2nd man:	He picks up the ball and throws it to Who
1st man:	Naturally.
2nd man:	Right.
1st man:	That's what I'm saying. Look. Bases are loaded. Somebody gets up to bat and hits a line drive to Who. Who throws to What. What throws to I-DON'T-KNOW. Triple play. Next batter gets up and hits a long ball to Why. Because, I don't know, he's on third and I don't give a darn.
2nd man:	What?
1st man:	I said I don't give a darn.
2nd man:	Hey, he's our shortstop.

BOXER SKIT

A = A T.V. interviewer, dressed in topcoat, with a hand-microphone.

B = The Boxer, who is wearing boxer shorts, boxing gloves, robe, and enters shadow-boxing and dancing around.

Enter A with B

A: Ladies and Gentlemen, tonight on ABC's Wild World of Sports, we take you into the ring here at Madison Square Garden for an on-the-spot chat with lower-East-Side's pride and joy. Rocky "Kid" Canvasback. Rocky, how do you like being on nationwide T.V.?

B: Hiya Mom! Hiya Dad! (Laughter)

A: What's so funny?

B: I'm an orphan.

A: Understand you have an outdoor bout in Montreal next February. Won't it be kind of cold?

B: No, we wear gloves.

A: By the way Rocky, how old are you?

B: 38 years old.

A: How did you get started in the fight business?

B: When I was a kid I was real tough. Could lick any kids on the block, except the Jones's. They were boys.

A: How many fights have you had?

B: 101. Won them all except the first 100. Got a winning streak going now.

A: Why did you quit the fight business?

B: Broke my hand.

A: Hitting an opponent I suppose?

B: No, the referee stepped on it.

A: By the way, how old did you say you were?

B: 52.

A: Fought a lot of people in your time, all kinds and sizes. What do you think of big men?

B: Big men eh, well, I think the bigger they are the harder they hit.

A: Tell us, Rocky, did you ever fight any of the world champs?

B: Yea, Mohammed Ali in the Olympic Arena. Had him really scared in the first round.

A: Really scared, huh? How come?

B: He thought he had killed me.

A: When you get knocked out like that, I suppose they carry you out on a stretcher, don't they?

B: No, I wear handles on my trunks.

A: How old?

B: 68.

A: Lot in the news about fixing fights, lately. Anybody ever ask you to throw one?

B: Yea, I remember when I was fighting Sugar Ray in Dallas, Texas. They asked me to take a dive in the sixth round.

A: But you didn't do it did you?

B: Nope, I never got that far.

A: Anything unusual ever happen?

B: Yea, remember the time I was fighting Honey Boy, Dave Lawrence in New York City. He smashed me right in the nose in the first round, but it didn't bleed until the fifth.

A: How come?

B: Tired blood.

A: Understand most boxers wear a mouth piece? Ever give you any trouble?

B: No, not usually, only when I'm eating.

A: How old are you?

B: 79. What's the matter you punchy or something?

A: Tell me, Rocky I've got a young kid, 14 years old, who wants to get into boxing. Have you got any advice for him?

B: You got a kid, yea . . . my advice, eat well, live clean, keep breathing, in and out, in and out, stop for more than three minutes you're a real goner. Then go around hitting people.

A: Any people?

B: No just little people, you see a kid, hit him, you see a dog, kick at it, good for the foot work. Live clean, hit hard, and keep breathing . . .

A: Give Rocky an exit.

THE FATAL QUEST

Characters:

The King
The Devoted Queen

The Handsome Duke
The Lovely Princess

The Curtains

The Kitten

> Directions: Lines are spoken exactly as written. Each character reads his stage directions as a part of his speech, and at the same time suits his action to his words. Ham acting is to be encouraged . . .

Act One

Curtain: The curtain rises for the first act.

Princess: The fair Princess stands at the window. She hears the distant sound of hoofs. "It is he," she cries, placing her hand upon her beating heart.

King: Enter the king.

Queen: Followed by the devoted Queen.

King: He seats himself on his throne, his scepter in his hand.

Queen: The Queen stands gracefully beside him, gazing at him fondly. "My Lord," she says in gentle tones. "why do you keep the Princess hidden from the eyes of men? Will wedlock never be hers?"

King: The King waxes stern. "Fair Queen," he says gruffly, "a thousand times have I repeated — the Princess shall become the wife of no man."

Duke: Enter the handsome Duke. "O King," he says in manly tones, "I have this morning a message of greatest importance."

Princess: The Princess enters at the left. At the sight of the handsome Duke she is startled. Her embarrassment increases her loveliness.

Duke: At first glance the Duke falls madly in love.

King: The King rises in excitement. "Speak," he shouts at the Duke, "and be gone."

Duke: The Duke gazes at the princess, his message forgotten.

Princess: The lovely maiden blushes and drops her eyes.

Queen: "Daughter," says the Queen, "why do you intrude yourself here without permission?"

Princess: The Princess opens her mouth to speak.

Duke: The Duke holds his breath.

Princess: "Alas," says the maiden in tones melting with sweetness, "my Angora kitten has strayed away and is lost."

Duke: "Fair Princess," cries the Duke in tones choked by feeling, "service for you were joy. The kitten I swear to find." With high courage he strides away.

King: "Stop him! Stop him!" shouts the King fiercely. "My servants shall find the cat for the Princess." Exit the King.

Queen: Followed by the devoted Queen.

Curtain: The curtain falls.

Act Two

Curtain: The curtain rises for the second act.

Princess: The fair Princess stands at the window. She hears the distant sound of hoofs. "It is he," she cries, placing her hand upon her beating heart.

King: Enter the King.

Queen: Followed by the devoted Queen.

Duke: The Duke steps in buoyantly, puss in arms.

Princess: "My kitten, my kitten," cries the Princess joyously. She takes her pet in her arms but her eyes follow the stalwart form of the Duke.

King: The King is pierced with jealousy.

Duke: The Duke falls upon his knees before the King. "O King," he says manfully, "I have found the kitten! I have come to claim the reward . . . the hand of the Princess."

King: The King trembles with wrath. "Be gone," he shouts furiously. "The hand of the Princess shall be won by no cat."

Duke: The Duke departs. As he passes the Princess, he grasps her soft hand. "I will return," he whispers in her ear.

Princess: The Princess does not speak, but her clear blue eyes reflect the secret of her soul.

Curtain: The curtain falls.

Act Three

Curtain: The curtain rises for the third and fatal act.

King: The King stands morosely in the center of the stage.

Queen: The Queen stands sadly beside him. "My Lord," she says in pleading tones, "relent. The Princess weeps day and night, nor will she be comforted."

King: The King turns his back. "Hold your peace!" he says in harsh tones.

Queen: The Queen weeps.

Duke: Enter the Duke, his sword at his side. "Oh King," he says in white passion, "for the last time I ask you for the hand of your daughter."

King: The King spurns him. "Be gone," he shouts once more.

Duke: The Duke draws his sword and stabs the King.

King: The King gasps and dies.

Queen: "My Lord, My Lord," cries the Queen passionately, and she falls dead upon the King.

Duke: "Great Caesar's Ghost, what have I done!" cries the Duke in anguish. He drinks a cup of poison and falls dead.

Princess: Hearing the cry, the Princess enters. She stops transfixed at the horrible sight before her. "Heaven help me," she cries, waving her shapely arms. "I die of grief." She falls dead upon the breast of her beloved.

King: Wee, wee, the King of the Land is dead.

Queen: Alas, alas, the devoted Queen is dead.

Princess: The Princess is dead, and beautiful even in death.

Curtain: The curtain falls.

Postlude

Curtain: The curtain rises for the postlude.

King: The King is still dead.

Duke: The manly Duke is still dead.

Queen: The devoted Queen is still dead.

Princess: The beautiful Princess is still dead and still beloved.

Curtain: The curtain falls forever.

THE STORY OF BEAUTIFUL BESSIE

This skit can be done two ways. Either divide your entire group into ten small groups or have ten individual kids come to the front of the room and make the sound effects below. The narrator reads the following story and whenever he gets to one of the names listed below, whoever is assigned that name (one person or small group) yells out the proper sound effect. At the end of the story when reader says "Ride 'em Cowboy" the entire group is told to jump up and each do his part in mass.

Rattlesnakes — hiss rattle, rattle, hiss rattle, rattle
Cowboys — yippee
Bessie — screams (Boy)
Love — coo-o-o-o
Bandits — Grr-r-r-r
Horses — stamp feet
Cattle — moo-o-o-o-o
Guns — bang, bang
Wolves — yow-o-o-o-o
Villain — Ah-h-h-h-h--h-h-h-Hah-h-h-h

STORY:

There was once a handsome cowboy . . . named Bill Jones, who lived far, far out West on a great ranch. He spent most of his days riding the range on a fine black horse . . . named Napoleon, and following his herds of bawling white-faced cattle . . .

On an adjoining ranch lived beautiful Bessie . . . Brown with her aged parents. All the cowboys . . . loved Bessie . . . but especially did the heart of the handsome Bill go pitter-patter when he looked into her eyes which were limpid pools of darkness. The bold bandit . . . Two Gun Sam also did feign to win the heart of beautiful Bessie . . . but she spurned his love . . .

One day Bessie's father and mother received a letter asking them to come to town at once for the bad villain . . . was about to foreclose on the mortgage to their ranch. Mr. Brown hitched up the horses . . . they put their guns . . . in the wagon, and Mrs. Brown placed her rattlesnake . . . charm in her purse, and they drove away to town.

"Ahh-g — Haa," cried the bold bandit . . . Two Gun Sam, when they were out of sight; for he had forged the letter. "Now, I shall have the love . . . of the Beautiful Bessie . . . So he rode his horse . . . up to the house, shot both of his guns . . . Beautiful Bessie . . . ran out of the house to see if someone had killed a wolf . . . or a rattlesnake . . .

When the girl saw Two Gun Sam, she started to run for her horse . . . But the bold bandit . . . grabbed her by the wrist. "Ah, proud beauty," said he. "You shall be my wife and someday I shall own all of your father's cattle . . . "

"Never," said Bessie . . . "I do not love . . . you."

"Then perhaps, you would rather be taken to a den of rattlesnakes . . . or eaten by the wolves . . . or trampled by the cattle . . . "

"Ah, yes, anything rather than let you steal my love . . . and take my father's cattle . . . " "Unhand me, you villain . . . "

"Very well, proud beauty, to the rattlesnakes . . . we go." And he put her on a horse . . . and started to speed away.

Gun . . . shots rang out, and the two bullets went through the top of the bold bandit's . . . sombrero. "Stop, villain . . . !, rattlesnake . . . wolf . . . " It was the handsome cowboy . . . Bill Jones.

97

When Two Gun . . . Sam saw the cowboy . . . he muttered to himself, "Coises, foiled again." He dropped Beautiful Bessie . . . from his horse . . . threw his gun . . . away and started for the hills where the wolves . . . and rattlesnakes . . . and cattle . . . roam, for he knew he would never win the love . . . of Bessie . . . nor get her father's cattle . . .

The handsome cowboy . . . looked into the eyes of the beautiful Bessie . . . which were still limpid pools of darkness and they both forgot about the wolves . . . and the rattlesnakes . . . and the villain . . . who wanted Mr. Brown's cattle . . .

Bessie . . . thanked the handsome cowboy . . . for rescuing her from the bold bandit . . . and she told Bill that she had been saving her love . . . for him. So they rode off together on their horses . . .

"RIDE EM COWBOY!"

CARRYING A CASE TO COURT. (Four short sequences)

Fellow comes through carrying a case with some bottles in it.

Mc: Where ya going with that?

Guy: Oh, I'm just taking a case to court.

Come through second time with case and stepladder.

Mc: Where ya going now?

Guy: Oh, I'm taking this case to a higher court.

Third time he comes through with a girl.

Mc: Where ya going now?

Guy: Oh, I'm just going to court.

Finally guy comes through with long underwear on.

Mc: What's now?

Guy: Lost my suit.

9. FUND RAISERS

9. FUND RAISERS

ROCKATHON

Here's a great idea that involves everyone in the group and serves as a project too. It's a twenty-four "Rockathon." Each participant signs up sponsors for 25¢ for every hour he rocks on his rocking chair. Here are the rules:

1. Everyone provides his own rocking chair.
2. Each participant must rock at least four hours in succession.
3. Time breaks only allowed for trips to the bathroom.
4. The chair must be moving at all times.

Hold the event in a large room and supply plenty of T.V.s, record players, radios, coffee, cookies and lemonade. Keep the participants awake by cheering, and a lot of cold, wet towels. Meals may be provided by the church, families or whatever. After participants finish rocking, they are given an official time certificate to show their sponsor. Keep a master record on all participants and their times to make sure all sponsor's money is collected. Take a lot of pictures, invite television to film the event. Also, keep track of total money raised every four or five hours and announce it to the kids. It keeps enthusiasm high.

101

RECIPE FUND RAISER

The youth group collects recipes from anyone in or out of the church, organizes them into sections and prints them with contributor's name at the bottom of the page. The recipes are mimeographed or speed printed and put in a semi-hard or hard cover notebook. Depending on the amount of recipes, sell them for $1.50 to $3.00 per book. Women are always looking for recipes and these will sell fast.

Recipe Form

Your Name: _____

Address and Phone Number: _____

_____

Title of Recipe: _____

Category: _____
              (soup, main dish, dessert, etc.)

INGREDIENTS:

PREPARATION:

YIELD:

TEA TIME FUND RAISER

Sometimes people get tired of youth selling tickets, or going to fund raising banquets, carwashes, bake sales, etc. So here's a different approach: Mail each church member a letter stating "We know you are tired of fund raisers, offering pitches, etc . . . so sit back, take off your shoes, relax, and have a cup of tea on us . . ." In each envelope you place a tea bag. Also ask the church member . . . "while you are relaxing, we'd like you to think about your youth group and consider helping them with their special project . . . (etc. etc.)" Casually ask for a donation, but make it as soft sell as possible. One group raised $800 with this approach and got many compliments.

AN EGG SALE

A surprisingly easy way to help youth earn money is with eggs. You begin by going to a home and asking the person there if she will donate an egg to help your youth group earn money (then tell her what the cause). Usually anyone will give an egg. After you have the egg, you go next door and ask that person if they will buy an egg to help your youth group earn money. Have no set price, just take whatever she will give you. Most often the egg will bring a quarter, although sometimes it might only bring a nickel or dime. Whatever the case, though, all money given is profit, and you might be amazed at how a group of youth can pile up profits quickly.

FUND RAISING OR FAMILY FUN

Put on the "World's Craziest Basketball Game," featuring the kids (youth group) versus the adults of the church (over 25). Sell tickets, award door prizes, have concessions, the whole works. The game will prove to be a lot of laughs and good for involving families in some great fellowship. Make it an annual affair and watch the attendance and excitement grow.

PANCAKE WASH

Have a pancake breakfast run concurrently with a carwash. People pay one price for both. They bring their car in, for a wash, then while they are waiting, go inside the church for a pancake breakfast. When they return, their car is finished. A very successful fund raiser.

10. CAMPING

10. CAMPING

CREATIVE WEEKEND RETREATS

If your group is in a rut when it comes to camping, here are some fresh new suggestions that can really make your weekends exciting and productive. The great thing about these suggestions is they can be held anywhere from a conference center to the basement of a house.

Weekend of Silence — The purpose of the weekend is to read scripture, meditate and enjoy listening to and watching God's creation. Each participant must refrain from talking or communicating the entire time. Caution: This kind of activity requires mature or serious minded participants who know in advance what is required there.

Discipline of Silence — Without a doubt, one of the most meaningful and effective times you can have at any conference is a ten to thirty minute discipline of silence. A discipline of silence requires the entire group to refrain from any conversation or communication with anyone. For best effectiveness, we suggest the following:

1. The best time is immediately after an evening meeting.

2. The Discipline of Silence should be announced by the speaker as part of his message.

3. The presentation must be positive so that the campers see it as a tool to help them rather than another ridiculous rule.

4. It should not be announced ahead of time.

5. Discipline of Silence should not be done for a weekend camp. At a week long camp, it should come sometime toward the last part of the week.

6. The campers should be asked to go somewhere outside unless they want to talk to one of their counselors or leaders. The counselors should be in their cabins and the leaders in the meeting hall. It should be announced that when someone goes in a cabin or meeting hall, it is because he wants help.

Weekend of Study — A great time of fellowship and everyone gets their homework done. Everyone brings homework, term papers, projects and uses the weekend getting his work done together.

Minority Weekend — Here is an effective way to let your group get a glimpse of what it is like to be the object of prejudice. The group is divided into two sub-groups. Each sub-group plays the role of a minority group for half of the weekend.

Service Weekend — Your kids need to give as well as get and this suggestion is a great giving experience. Group spends an entire weekend at an old folks home. This is not just an exercise in patronizing, but in listening, understanding and helping.

SPECIALIZED CAMPS

1. TRAVEL CAMP

   Travel camps or caravan camps are simply experiences in group camping with a new location every day. The campers travel in buses, campers, stationwagons, or cars, even bikes. Depending on the time allowed, each day's schedule consists of some travel time, some sightseeing and a meeting. Some days may just be sightseeing and activities. The following is an eight day travel schedule: (fill in your locations and other specifics).

   FRIDAY
   > Load in San Diego at 4:00 p.m.
   > Travel 550 miles to Zion National Park

   SATURDAY — ZION NATIONAL PARK
   > Arrive at 12:00 at Zion
   > Sleep
   > Free Time
   > Campfire

   SUNDAY — ZION NATIONAL PARK
   > Sunday service — invite campers
   > Free Time
   > Evening campfire

MONDAY — ZION NATIONAL PARK
  Morning Bible Study
  Hike and Swim
  Free Time
  Campfire

TUESDAY — BRYCE CANYON NATIONAL PARK
  Bible Study
  Leave ZION at 9:00 a.m.
  Arrive BRYCE at 1:00 p.m.
  Free Time
  Campfire

WEDNESDAY — SALT LAKE CITY, UTAH
  Bible Study
  Leave BRYCE at 8:00 a.m.
  Arrive SALT LAKE CITY 4:00 p.m.
  Evening Service

THURSDAY — SALT LAKE CITY, UTAH
  Bible Study
  Visit Mormon Temple Square
  Free Time
  Evening Meeting

FRIDAY — SALT LAKE CITY, UTAH
  Bible Study
  Swim in the Great Salt Lake
  Free Time
  Leave for San Diego (810 miles)

SATURDAY — SAN DIEGO
  Arrive 12:00 p.m.
  Collapse! ! !

The important thing to notice about a travel camp is the flexibility of the schedule. You play it by ear during the day. You let the location determine what your activities will be. If you are tired then you sleep in. This is a great opportunity to get close to a group of kids.

2. WATER SKI TRIP

This conference is a "one-on-one" week long camp-out by a lake, large river or bay. To attend, a prospect must attend two orientation meetings. The meetings cover basic steps in sharing Christ and a list of questions.

The first meeting covers the basic steps in sharing Christ. The second meeting the class discusses a questionnaire that was given to them the previous week. Each student is to research and find answers. After the discussion a test is given and people with the highest scores are eligible to attend. However, they must bring a non-Christian in order to finally be accepted.

A. The schedule is simple: Water ski, breakfast, water ski, lunch, water ski, dinner, water ski, meeting, sleep.

The speaker simply talks around the campfire at night and asks those who are interested in knowing more to meet in a certain area. The speaker may help but the bulk of the responsibility is on the Christian who brought his friend.

B. Where do you get the boats?

First of all, you need one boat per ten campers. Recruit boats from church members, outside people or anyone who has a boat and is willing to go. You should pay **all** their expenses.

C. What about food?

Don't skimp on food. The best arrangement is to set up "cook-groups" of about 10-12 kids. Each group elects a cook captain. He is responsible to see that his group has enough cooking utensils, barbecue grill, etc. for his group. Each camper brings his own eating utensils and washes his own dishes. There is a control kitchen tent. The food is given out at certain times. It is given to the captains **only.**

D. Cost

Even with good quality food, you can usually keep the costs quite low. The important thing is that your costs cover the expenses, because a water ski trip will not be difficult to fill with kids anxious to pay the price.

3. OVERNIGHT CAMP OUT

This is a simple camp. For example, camp at a campground near a beach on Friday night. For dinner have hamburgers, cakes, etc. (keep simple). The rest of the evening may be a campfire ghost story, games, songs, devotion can be led by one of the kids or the youth director. Saturday morning have breakfast rolls, or donuts, juice and milk. Spend the day at the beach, have hot dogs for lunch and go home Saturday night.

4. MEXICO TRIP (Boys only — fill in your own specifics)

A two day to one week excursion to the coast of Mexico with guys. The entire day is spent surfing, skin diving, cycling, loafing. Be sure to provide plenty of excellent food. Have one meeting per night with a real manly speaker (ex-football player, etc.) who has participated with the guys.

Night Rocket Fight: (This can only be done in Mexico or where firecrackers are legal). Give each boy a supply of rockets and divide into 2 teams. One team barricades itself in some kind of fort or hideout. The other team attacks. Rockets are thrown at each other until supply runs out. Some groups provide each boy with cheap plastic goggles. The rockets are almost harmless but could be considered too dangerous by some. But they sure are fun! (Rockets may be bought in Tijuana and are very inexpensive.)

5. SNOW SKI TRIP — three days

This is another "one-to-one" conference with the same requirements for attendance as the water ski trip. A good time to schedule this would be Monday through Wednesday of Christmas vacation.

Try to book a chalet dormitory. It is much cheaper than any ski club. The equipment may be rented and you can instruct dry-land lessons or many kids learn at school. (Of course, out there in snow country, everyone knows how to ski, anyway.)

6. PACK-IN

The leader should be a person who is well liked by the guys and is a man's man type. Take a group of guys to some high altitude mountains and climb like crazy. You can bring all Christians and work on developing leadership or you can make it a "one-on-one" trip.